In memory of Grandma Bowgen 1911-2005, with love **H.C.**

Text by Mary Joslin
Illustrations copyright © 2006 Helen Cann
This edition copyright © 2006 Lion Hudson

The moral rights of the author and illustrator
have been asserted

A Lion Children's Book
an imprint of
Lion Hudson plc
Mayfield House, 256 Banbury Road,
Oxford OX2 7DH, England
www.lionhudson.com
ISBN-13 978 0 7459 4990 1
ISBN-10 0 7459 4990 8

First edition 2006
1 3 5 7 9 10 8 6 4 2 0

A catalogue record for this book is available
from the British Library

Typeset in 17/19 Venetian 301 BT
Printed and bound in Singapore

On that
Easter Morning

Mary Joslin
Illustrated by Helen Cann

LION
CHILDREN'S

The children clapped their hands and waved palm branches.
'Jesus is coming!' they shouted gleefully. 'Jesus is coming to Jerusalem for the Passover, just like we are!'

The grown-ups were equally thrilled. 'If Jesus is coming to the capital city for the most important festival of the year,' they whispered, 'then he must be about to do something spectacular. Perhaps he is going to declare himself king and make us a free again.'

'God bless the king!' shouted someone. At once, the whole crowd joined in.

'God bless the king! God bless the one who comes in God's name! Alleluia!'

At the centre of the joyful uproar, Jesus and his disciples made their way along the road. Jesus was riding a donkey and waving at the crowds as if they were all his friends.

They went up to the city and into the Temple courtyard. It was like a marketplace, with everyone getting ready for the festival. Traders were shouting, customers were haggling. Jesus gazed at the scene with anger and disbelief. Then he sprang into action!

'This is meant to be a house of prayer,' he called. 'Get out at once!'

With surprising strength, Jesus began overturning the tables and driving out the animals that were for sale. Coins jingled on the paving stones. Pigeons flew to the sky in a noisy whirr of wings.

The religious leaders glowered disapprovingly. 'It's that preacher from Galilee,' they muttered. 'He claims to be telling people about God and God's kingdom. He's just a troublemaker... and a dangerous one at that.'

Then everything seemed to go quiet. Jesus spent his days preaching, as he always did.

He asked his disciples to make arrangements for them all to share a Passover meal together.

On the chosen evening, they met in an upstairs room. Jesus stood up, took off his coat and tied a towel around his waist. Then he fetched a bowl of water and began washing his disciples' feet, just as a servant would.

'I am your teacher and your leader,' he explained, 'but I have acted as your servant. I want you to follow my example and serve one another.

'Tonight, I am giving you a new commandment: As I have loved you, so you must love one another.'

The Passover supper was always more than a meal. It was a time for the people to remember how, long ago, God had rescued them from their enemies and led them to a land where they could live in peace.

While they were eating, Jesus took a piece of bread, gave a prayer of thanks, broke it, and gave it to his disciples. 'Take and eat it,' he said; 'this is my body.'

Then he took the wine cup, gave thanks to God, and gave it to them. 'Drink it, all of you,' he said; 'this is my blood.'

He went on to explain that God was going to make a new promise to his people. He said that his body was going to be broken and his blood was going to be shed; yet because of his suffering, his followers would be able to enter into God's kingdom.

At the end of the evening, Jesus and his disciples left Jerusalem to find shelter for the night. They walked across the valley to an olive grove known as the Garden of Gethsemane.

Once they were deep in the shadows, Jesus gathered them together. 'You wait here,' he said. 'I want to be alone to pray.'

As he disappeared into the darkness, one of the disciples noticed something.

'Judas Iscariot isn't here.'

'He slipped out earlier,' replied one.

'I think it was something to do with money,' replied another. 'He'll know where to find us, in the usual place. We might as well try to grab some sleep.'

They were barely awake when Judas returned. He was leading a large crowd of armed men. Judas had betrayed Jesus to his enemies, and they were coming to arrest him.

Jesus was taken to a great council of priests and teachers of the Law, their faces lit by a hundred flickering lamps.

'The things you have been preaching to others are dangerous,' they accused him. 'They go against our most sacred beliefs and traditions. Your teaching is a crime against God!'

Even though they could not find any proof of their accusations, the religious leaders were determined to get rid of Jesus.

In the morning, they led him to the Roman governor of Jerusalem, Pontius Pilate. 'This man claims to be a king,' they told him.

Pilate was not convinced. However, what concerned him most was how to keep order in the city during the festival. He decided to appeal to the crowd outside his palace. 'It is the custom for me to free a prisoner at Passover time,' he announced. 'Shall I set this man free?'

The crowd that was waiting was in an angry mood.

'Crucify him! Crucify him!' they shouted. Fearing a riot, Pilate agreed.

The Roman soldiers jeered at their prisoner.

'Call yourself a king?' they jeered. 'Welcome to your coronation!'

They draped a cloak around him as if he were the emperor himself and they pressed a crown of thorns onto his head. Then they beat him and hit him till he was worn out by their violence.

When they had had their fun, they loaded a wooden cross onto Jesus' shoulders and forced him to carry it to the hill called Calvary which lay just outside the city walls

There they nailed Jesus to the cross and raised it into position on the hilltop. Two criminals were crucified on either side.

Jesus said a prayer: 'Forgive them, Father, they don't know what they are doing.'

As he hung there, the sky turned dark and the air grew cold.

Meanwhile, a man named Joseph, who was from the town of Arimathea, had gone to plead with Pilate to let him take Jesus' body.

The late afternoon sun shone weakly as he came to the place of execution to collect it. He wrapped it in a linen sheet and laid it on a funeral stretcher.

A sorrowful little procession of Jesus' friends gathered. They carried the body to Joseph's rock-cut tomb. Gently they laid it on a ledge in the dark cave before hurrying to roll the huge stone door in place.

They had no time for the usual funeral customs. The sun was nearly setting, and the blood-red sky was a reminder that the sabbath day of rest was about to begin.

When the sabbath was over, very early on the Sunday morning, the group of women who had been at Jesus' burial went back to the tomb. They wanted to wrap the body in the proper way, with sweet-smelling spices among the folds of linen.

To their dismay, they found the stone door rolled away. Cautiously they stepped inside.

'The body isn't here,' one of them whispered. 'I remember exactly where they put it.'

Then they saw them: two figures in shining clothes were standing there in the dim light.

'Why are you looking among the dead for someone who is alive?' they asked. 'Jesus is not here; he has been raised to life.'

The women hurried away to tell their astonishing news to the disciples.

'The body has gone,' they explained. 'We don't know where it is.'

The one named Mary Magdalene persuaded two of them, Peter and John, to go and see for themselves.

John ran faster and reached the tomb first, but Peter came racing up behind and went straight in.

It was just as they had been told: the body had gone. All that was left were the linen wrappings.

The two men stepped outside into the dawn light. As the sky paled from grey to pearl, hope rose in their hearts. Perhaps the news was true. Perhaps Jesus really was alive.

Mary Magdalene stayed by the tomb, weeping. As she peered inside, she saw two angels.

'Why are you crying?' they asked her.

'They have taken away the body of Jesus,' she said. 'I know where they have put him.'

She turned round as she heard a voice and saw a figure silhouetted against the sky. 'Why are you crying?' asked the person. 'Who are you looking for?'

It must be the gardener, thought Mary. 'Oh, sir,' she said, 'if you took the body away, please tell me where I can go and find it.'

'Mary,' came the only answer.

Then she knew: she was looking at Jesus himself.

The sun rose, shining gold in the clear blue sky. Mary knew for sure that there was good news for all of Jesus' friends and followers.

Jesus was alive again: not a king in this world, but the king of heaven itself.

The dark power of death was defeated. God's own love lit the world on that Easter morning.